I

SPEAK

FOR

THOSE

WHO

HAVE

ALREADY

SPOKEN

I Speak for Those Who Have Already Spoken
Copyright © 2021 by David Piper

Author photograph by Machiko Kyoya

Cover design by Mona Z. Kraculdy

All rights reserved. No part of this book can be reproduced in any form by any means without written permission. Please address inquiries to the publisher:

www.thetherabooks.com

ISBN: 978-0-578-98313-4

Library of Congress Control Number: 2021947236

A Thera Books First Edition, September 2021

Printed in the United States of America

I SPEAK FOR THOSE WHO HAVE ALREADY SPOKEN

DAVID PIPER

A Poetry by the People feature series selection

THERA BOOKS
Sacramento, California
SAY | SOMETHING

For Machiko Kyoya, wife, friend, and lover

The words I seek do not exist.
They lay somewhere in our spiritual bliss.
But this is to you from me, who began in one day.

—David Alexander, the last of the *Red-Hot Pipers ... Zoom ...!*

CONTENTS

Backstory 1
Let Me Speak 3
I Am the Drum 4
Black Top 5
An Og 6
Uncle J.B. Told Me 8
John Thunder 9
Amadou Bamba 11
Heru Ptah 12
Last Poets 13
Amadou Bamba to Ntozake Shange 14
Amadou Bamba 17
Poet 22
Shake the Sphere 25
Got to Lead 26
We Know 27
Gone Ahead 28
One Note 31
Donnelle McGee 32
Civil Rights War/Rap Brown 33
Fred Hampton 34
Rodney King 36
Huey P. 37
God Blessed America 39
Jim Crow 45
Back Porch 46
Round Midnight 47

Jazz Is	48
Tamara & Jay's New Addition	49
I Went to College	51
Eastern Sun	52
Four Women	53
I Got Jokes	58
Song On	59
Drummer's Son	60
Tribute	61
About the Author	62

BACKSTORY

I was born post war 1943 San Francisco, CA, raised in Dallas Texas. My mother was a single parent assisted by her mother and grandmother. She gave birth to three of us and only two survived, my sister and me. Bearing the burden of two children and Jim Crow laws of the South, she provided as much of a living as possible. I parented my sister until she reached the age of 5 years. We were then separated by an "unscheduled event." Unbeknownst to either of us, the adults had arranged to change our destiny for whatever their reasons may have been. I was awaken in the early hours of a Friday morning, told I would not be attending school that day and would be leaving with these strange people sitting in the kitchen. One identified himself as my father, the other two were his sister and her husband. I was into my mid teen years (14) when I met my father, and of course it was way too late for bonding. I understood later that it was at the beckoning of my mother, he and his older sister arrived from San Francisco that day, and packed up my few possessions and transported me to San Francisco, CA. I learned in the five days we were together traveling toward San Francisco from Texas that he was already married and had other children. I met my stepbrothers, my father's wife, her sister's husband all in a matter of one week. That was the beginning and end of our relationship. I never saw my brothers nor their mother again. Aunt Ethel and Uncle Roy became my surrogate parents immediately. My father would come by for a few minutes at a time for the first couple of months and then fewer and fewer times up until no visits at all. I never missed not knowing my father because the minute Uncle Roy came into my life, I realized a man had stepped up. Yeah, he was hard and strict but he more than filled my father's shoes; he would instill in me life-long lessons that helped me become the man I am today. Aunt Ethel and Uncle Roy guided me through high school and the first years of college. I am very much indebted to them as they paved the path that allowed me to launch my life with a supportive foundation.

LET ME SPEAK

People often ask me, "What is it that you do, brotha?" And I often say, when I have to describe myself. I am a JaliyaTOLOGIST."

A Jali, concerned with the origins of JaliyaOLOGY. JaliyaOLOGY being a scientific methodology for analyzing social situations. So, that makes me a scientist that analyzes social conditions through the vehicle of JaliyaOLOGY.

The best way to tell if something is scientific or not, is to look at the end of the title or the word. As soon as you see OLOGY or OLOGIST at the end of the title or the word, then you know it's scientific.

I AM THE DRUM

I am the drum
I am as old as time
I have the rhythm.
If you have the rhyme
My people of the sun, taken by a hostile hand
They even tried to silence me-the pulse of the Motherland
But you see, the bond is too strong, and so I live on
Through space and time as a vibe
My beat unifies-making people dance, chant and sing
All day and all night.
I ignite the fires of the Ancient Flame
Connecting with the Ancestors, revealing their reign
This energy continues through our generational line
There is no rhythm greater than mine.

BLACK TOP

It's the black top brotha
You come ready or you don't come at all

AN OG

Dr. P

Let me start with my essential

An OG with academic credentials

San Francisco, Third street 'N Palou

You on the corner, you don't know what to do

I used to walk into libraries take the tray down

You say a word, it was academic spray down

I was quick, undaunted by hard times

I knew my facts, it's all 'bout be on time

All the phonies, liars and pretendos

Co-opted, corrupted, skewed by innuendoes

Living that life titled societal misfit

Fast lanin but let me flip the switch

Dr. P don't try to be somebody else

I 'm here to give you tools, be yourself

Life is but a labyrinth you need a map

Listen to the message now that's a rap

UNCLE J.B. TOLD ME

Black is a label
An unfounded fable
A lifetime warranty of free will disabled

Brown is around with a distinction profound rooted in the ability
To morph wherever it is found

White is a socially constructed narcissistic delusional
State of grandeur a concocted concept baited to allure

Yellow, from the minds of an instant teller
Got to be mellow if it's going to be stellar
When the Eastern sun rises it's a different fellow

Red, treaties read you're not being mislead
Discovered by the founders, stopped in its tracks
To get my bounce I'm trying to get back
Indigenous Ned damn near dead

JOHN THUNDER

Americans of the united state

Could it be you arrived a little too late

How came ye to claim occupied land

How in your wisdom did you not understand

Who heard the indigenous cry

Who saw great Jordan roll

Did you feel the chariot swing low

The trouble I see nobody knows

There is a wide-wide wonder in the fall

That from degraded rest and servile toil

Europe's discard brought liberty and just us all

The fiery spirit of the discoverers unknown unnamed

Has left a rugged path and a bloody stain

Land where our people died

Land of pilgrim pride

Oh say can't you see

AMADOU BAMBA

A people born

With the sun or moon in their face

Earth surrounding their limbs

Water connected to their bodies

Plants as a part of their meal

Understand the spirit of life

And never misinterpret the conversation

HERU PTAH

Listen, the answers that we seek are always within the questions that we ask.

The questions that always seem to pop up for me are:

- Why am I?
- Who I am?
- When I am being
- What I am
- Where I am?
- Is there life after death?
- And is seven really up?

And deeper still, why do people think that they exist for some purpose or reason?
Existentialism is usually explained in reference to something else's existence.
For example, most often people explain existence as a byproduct of some kind of Divine Creator:
This kind of explanation takes for granted
That they exist because some other/thing wanted them to exist.
There are those who will not grant the existence of the Universal Designer as a starting point
They contend that *Is just Is*
For you to say you don't believe in a Universal Designer
Says that you recognize there is a Universal Designer

LAST POETS

Alright now, I've got just the thing for you.
The question is what chu gon' do?
I've got black ones, brown ones, red ones, yellow ones too
I've even got the right one made especially for you
Yeah, twentyfo eight will make you late.
Tain't no doubt
Know what I'm talking about
Been reading them scheme books.
Page number four, how not to get took.
When I step up into the place ay yo, I step correct. Woo-Hah! Woo-Hah! Got you all in check! I talk that head nod shit, make you break your neck!
Brotha whatchu you mean it ain't slick?
This is the latest in getting rich quick.
So step up, step up and try your luck.
These black ones will take off the pounds
With these browns ones you can really get down
The red ones will take you to the ground
And the yellow will bring you back around.
Now them right ones will make you strut your stuff
Spin you around, touch the ground and call anybody's bluff
When I step up into the place ay yo, I step correct. Woo-Hah! Woo-Hah! Got you all in check! I talk that head nod shit, make you break your neck! Throw your hands up in the air, don't ever disrespect!
Yo yo Blood! I got just the thing to do!
It only   cost you

AMADOU BAMBA TO NTOZAKE SHANGE

My Great Great Grandmother was a spiritualist. And she knew all about the manifestation of trance, healing, and visions found in spirit and raps that were as easy to git as a handful of herbs or three revelations. When she transitioned into the 40 million spirits, critturs and celestial bodies, she left me to ponder life and explore the purpose of existence. In 1968, as I began to ponder life and explore the purpose of existence, I took up my Great Great Grandmother's trade. 'Cuz I figured with all this calamitous power, I could make myself white just like everybody else. I could go to a white private school, get myself a good white education, and make myself some big white money. Now the part I overlooked was what would any self-respecting, Al Kebulan Spiritualist do with such an outlandish bequest. And therein lies the rub. White isn't a person, white isn't a place, white isn't a country, white isn't even where you have a know exactly what to do wife, two forever happy children, nice house, a Cadillac car and grass for the children to cut so they can earn some white spending money.

White is a socially constructed narcissistic delusional state of grandeur, a concocted concept baited to allure. What was I going to do believing in this kind of illusion? How would I render myself fit, suitable, adaptable? How would I acclimate, assimilate, accommodate? I didn't even know about triple AAA insurance. Even if I went around making other people white, on the spot, using my Great Great grandmother's manifestation of healing, visions, trance, and raps that were as easy to git as a handful of herbs or three revelations found in spirit; this spiritual thang was gon become politically dangerous for the 41 million spirits, critturs and celestial bodies on my side. A delusion is incompatible with an illusion. Neither compliments the other. Both forgo the facts that now you see me, now you don't mess with me. I come from a long line of retired sorcerers, active houngans and penny ante fortune tellers.

I have some herbs and three revelations. One, all things are possible, two, nothing is absolute, and three, everything happens in time. But ain't no Al Kebulan Spiritualist in their right mind gon' make you white. This is a technicolor dilemma you looking at.

Come on and live my life wid me for a minute. I didn't want certain moments at all. I'd give them to anybody.

You come wid me when in 1954, I tried to integrate the public schools in Dallas, TX. You, git wid me now, we can both be the little red niggah in an all-white school. I even tried to make friends at the YMCA's summer camp. But I was always a little too dark, lips a little too full, hair entirely too nappy; a mistake in racial integrity, an error in white folks' most absurd fantasies. Be the Negro child in 1958 who was not dark enuf to lovingly ignore, not beautiful enuf to leave alone, not smart enuf to move outta the way, not bitter enuf to die at an early age. Shange, I live your life every day home girl, and I don't want certain moments, I don't want certain moments at all, I'd give them to anybody.

AMADOU BAMBA

I began my writing career by telling lies on paper, 'cause, in school, when they want to know what you did on your summer vacation and you have never heard that word in your house, lest of all know how to spell it. You invent shit. You tell the class about *New York New York the big apple. Sixteen million feet nationals, florsheims, tom mccanns stepping on each other rejoicing over the death of one nigger toe. Cold callous feet trotting up and down synthetic avenues, streets, boulevards* ... You create notes from your mother informing the teacher why you were absent, all that week: hell your great, great, great, Uncle Willie died again that week. And it was profitable too. 'Cause the school would collect money for the funeral and give it to you. My whole family died in that tornado last Monday and I was rich, for a minute. You see, this Ms. Mary Katherine, she never did like me, you know what I'm saying. She would always want to question me, trying to shake the validity of my story. She cum talking 'bout, "you have your mother come to school with you tomorrow." Good thing for me my mother had died too 'else I would've been in big trouble. Then she cum asking, "how many times your mother is gon die," huh, how many times? Humpback Witch! Made me give back all the money.

I wrote letters to friends who had moved away to better housing, better schools, better states. By the time I finished telling about all the improvements in the neighborhood, I had everyone wishing they had stayed in Waxahachie.

Wait a minute now, don't be judging me. Naw, don't judge me. Check yourselves. What is this thing you call Fiction? Is it not creative lying, and acceptable? Look at the movies, what are they other than rearranged truths. Now, if you are so concerned with writing the truth, you should go into research and science where it is considered to be important. But if you are going to write history, literature, English, creative writing, spoken word, you had best learn how to gainfully lie. You see the issue becomes whether others believe what you're saying as opposed to whether it's true or not. An infamous philosopher of time once told me, "boy, a lie is as good as duh truf if'n somebody believes it." What I discovered about myself is that I can take a simple situation and add so many variables to it that people have a hard time not believing what I'm saying.

I remember when I was a youngster in Waxahachie on my uncle's farm. My cousin and me were roughhousing in my Auntie's living room and "accidently" knocked the lamp onto the floor. Well, what actually happened is, we was fighting and I grabbed the lamp from the table and threw it at him, but I missed. And of course, the lamp hit the wall and busted into a bunch of small pieces. My Auntie came into the room, saw the broken lamp and pieces scattered across the floor and she had a fit. She beat both of us up at the same time and then threatened us with "you wait 'till J.B. gets home." Well I wasn't scared of dat "...wait 'til J. B. gets home" speech. I knew that my mother didn't like my aunt nor her brotha JB, so I was ready for the "wait 'till your uncle hears about this" bit. When my mother came to pick me up, I met her in the front yard. Me and moms had this updated greeting that indicated the type of day we had experienced. She would always greet me with, "What it be like, David Jr.?" That was always a signal to me that she was having a good day. Now that line always left the door wide open for me to do my thing if I needed to, you see what I'm saying? And this was one of dem days that I needed to do my thing. So I said, "Ain't nothing happening, ain't a damn thing happening, other than uncle JB's dog died." See, when I use the words shit, damn or muthafucka she knows I'm trying to be grownup, so I must have had a bad day. 'Cause me trying to be grown up seem to always end up in an ass whupping. She looked me over for a minute and saw that I had been in some kind of scuffle or something and said, "the dog died, JB's dog died?" She sit down on the porch steps, put her purse down, and pulled me into her lap, "how did the dog die, baby?"

Me: "He found some dead Mule meat in the barn, he ate it and he died. With curiosity cropping the edges of her empathy she ask, "Some dead mule meat in the barn, how did dead mule meat get into the barn?"

Me: "The barn caught on fire, burned up the Mule, and the dog ate the meat and died." Mom: "The barn caught on fire, how, how did the barn catch on fire?"

Me: "It was the sparks from the house. You see the roof of the house was burning and the sparks flew over to the barn, burned up the barn and the Mule and the dog ate the meat and died."

Mom: "The house?" She had now eased me out of her lap and was standing, one foot on the ground and the other foot on the first step leading up to the porch.

Mom: looking at the house: "What do you mean the house? How did JB's house catch on fire!? Mom is in a panic now, she calls for my Auntie to come outside.

Mom: "Ethel Mae, Ethel Mae, what in the hell has been going on around here!? Did you hear what happened to these children today?"

Aunt Ethel: "So he told you what happened with the lamp?"

Mom: "The lamp?"

Me: "Yeah, It was the lamp. (I'm still cool and collected) The fire from the lamp caught on to the curtains and shot up the walls to the roof, the roof started burning and the sparks flew over to the barn, burned up the barn and the Mule and the dog ate the meat and died." Mom: "The lamp?"

Aunt: "What fire?"

The Dog: Wuff, wuff

Me: "Now look, (with all the childhood arrogance I could muster up) I'm not going to tell you this but one more time. The lamp was sitting on grandma's table. You see, and Auntie's son was throwing rocks at the mailman, when grandma found out about it she had a heart attack and passed out; that's when she bumped against the table, knocked over the lamp and, the fire from the lamp caught onto the curtain, shot up the walls to the roof, the roof started burning and the sparks flew over to the barn, burned up the barn and the mule and JB's dog ate the meat and died."

Mom: "But J.B's. house is right there, and I'm looking at the barn And the dog is barking at chu."

Me: "Well Alex Mae, who you gon believe, me or your lying eyes? That's when they both commenced to beat my ass. You see, that's the day I learned a lie is as good as the truth, if somebody believes it, but it is not the same as."

Sampled from *The Flip Wilson Show*

POET

I didn't start out to be a poet, because, poetry has been defined as feeling for the ear and for the eye. Some demand that it rhyme, others feel that interval and meaning are more important. Neither really matters to me because I didn't start out to be a poet. I wanted to write prose, prose that would live forever. So, every time I would write a line, supposedly a poem, I would find some prose. Then I would rush over to the professors at the University and show them my work. Well, I stopped doing that. 'cause they got too many rules about what it ain't, what you can't say and do with a poem. They would read my stuff and say, "you can't do that!" "You can't do this! No, no, no, no ..." And that's when I would get mad! Because, I already had!

I didn't start out to be a poet! Or they would read something I had written, trying to be myself, after having been somebody else for so many years, and always say something, something totally unrelated to what it was. I couldn't dig that, because, I didn't start out to be a poet. But I tried. I quoted PAUL LAWRENCE DUNBAR, and they objected to the use of dialect. I mentioned DU BOIS, and they said, "communist in hell." Well, M.B. TOLSON I rhapsodized, and they had never heard of him. So I screamed, "LANGSTON HUGHES YOU MUTHA FU...... That's when they put me out, said I wasn't ready. At the door I said, "Don't forget y'all, I didn't start out to be a poet, but I betcha I am!

During post war 1943, there was no one around to teach me about Melanin Endowed People who wrote poetry. I was taught the kind of poetry that none of us could understand. Like when I was in my sophomore year, the tenth grade, at Sacred Heart High School, San Francisco CA; most of the students there didn't even want to learn English. So, it didn't make sense to mention poetry. You say poetry to one of those Irish white boys, you just might get your ass kicked. So, in my English class this Jesuit Brother sneaked past the Irish white boys and dropped this book on the desk of the only two Melanin Endowed students in the class, sitting in the back. Me and Richard Jacks. Then he told us to read the poem on page eleven and tell the class what it meant. Jacks took to staring at me, I took to staring right back, then he said, "I'm not reading no poem and have them Irish white boys kick me in the ass." And thinking on these things, I paused and commenced to ponder the meaning of this significant moment. To be or what, that's the real question. Whether 'tis nobler in the mind to suffer the slings and arrows of outrageous fortune, or to take arms against a sea of troubles, And, by opposing, end them?" So I said, "well I guess it's alright, shit, I'll try it." I picked up the book and opened it to page eleven and read the poem. W HAT NO W UP SIDE T HE W ALL I SEE IT H T HE SHA DOW OF AN I MA GE ME. I looked at Jacks, I said, "damn let me read this again." W HAT NO W UP SIDE T HE W ALL I SEE IT H T HE SHA DOW OF AN I MA GE ME. I turned to Richard and said, "what the fuck?" So Richard said, "give me the book young brotha." "Give me the book Holmes." I gave him the book. Jacks took the book, stood up, walked past the Irish white boys to the front of the class, opened the book to page eleven, and read the poem. WHAT NOW? UPSIDE THE WALL, I SEEITH THE SHADOW OF AN IMAGE, ME! I said damn, Jacks. That was deep! Now you know what deep means don't you? When I say deep, I mean damn, I recognized all them words, individually. But I couldn't make any sense out of the order in which they currently appeared. But to make a long story long, I learned a lot about poetry. I learned that a good poem contains one of four elements: It tells a story. It paints a picture. It expresses an emotional experience. It reflects on life. The basic themes are: Love and hate. Birth and death. Human relationship to the environment. Human relationship to humans. The elements of a good poem seem always to be the common interest of everyone.

SHAKE THE SPHERE

To be or what
That's the real question
So be yourself
'cause everybody else is already taken

GOT TO LEAD

Who am I
A product the US wasted
Is it wrong
Is it true
I guess I know what I have to do
Can't stop now
Got to lead my people
Up amen Street
Down kingdom come steeple
We are African
And here we come
Some of y'all know
Where we're coming from
Not being free
To be myself
Always trying to be
Somebody else
Can't stop now
Got to lead my people
Up amen Street
Down kingdom come steeple

WE KNOW

We know who
And that doesn't tell us what
So why should when
Say anything about where

GONE AHEAD

All things are possible. Nothing is absolute. Everything
    happens in time. But ain't no Great Great Grandmother
    in her right mind gon leave you without light.
I am, who I am when I am being what I am, where I am.
Each time I visit
Each time I walk back into our lives
I wonder
Like any child pondering from time to time in the endless
    loop of dialogue
How did I get my identity?
Well now I know
I inherited it
It engulfed my being when my mother and small family
    moved in with her mother, her mothers' mother, my
    Great Great Grandmother

It was floating around the house
In the tales my Great Great Grandmother told to me
It was floating around the house
In the looks and non-looks
She afforded some people while not others
It was floating around
When she died and left it in the air to inundate someone

My mother's mother was too exhausted
My mother was submerged in working long hours
My Sista was too young

So it grabbed hold of me
I mean, there it was
41 million spirits, critters and celestial bodies
Wrapped up all around me

There were times when I would be immured by the senselessness of parental reasoning and find this woman, eyes deep, dark, clear, long coarse gray hair, deeply imbued brown skin, a face etched by the forbearance of time, of small but sturdy frame, settled in a chair doing what Great Great Grandmother are supposed to do, which is absolutely mystifying. Tuella Hickman would call me in a high tone, low moan, loud groan, soft grunt, hard funk voice into her room, light up her pipe, fill the air with that odor of purple leafed tobacco
And tell me a story
That always ended with the same sustenance, *Don't you want to be like that when you grow up, Dava junior?*
To which I would respond gleefully, "Yeah Granny, yeah!"
As we talked, our parent-child talk
Abandoned in the endless loop of dialogue
I would cross easily over into her point of view
Soaked up by that smaze in the air
Transformed from the limitations of four walls
To a universe where all things are possible, nothing is absolute, and everything happens in time 'Cause ain't no Great Great Grandmother in her right mind gon leave their Great-grandchild here ignorant!
I thought I heard a door close

Did someone come in? Did someone leave?
No steps, simply the closing of a door
I reach for the reassuring hand
It's not there
And then I hear that voice
Be here when the time comes and your time will be here
    when you're gone

I guess she's gone on ahead

ONE NOTE

I got pounds of emboldened tears
Songs ringing in my ears
The sound of a million voices sing
I cry for I feel the pain
I often just hear one keening note
D flat, C sharp tense, tight
I got sounds in my ears
Old sounds, emboldened tears

DONNELLE McGEE

There had to be one ship that bucked up out of the water
   and reversed its course back to Africa.

CIVIL RIGHTS WAR/RAP BROWN

A Brotha who had a heart and was really down
Was the Revolution's spokesman H. Rap Brown
He was talking about the truth in such a soulful way
That the power structure wanted to put Rap away
Waking people up was the Brotha's aim
But the people seem to think it was all a game
People used to say, *Man that cat can rap*
But no one seems to care where our brotha's at
The fact that Rap is gone doesn't bother some
That's because they never knew where he was coming from
Since this righteous brotha is gone, we should not fall back
And we could start by asking questions 'bout our Brotha Rap
The message that he brought to the people's ears
Gave us courage and the strength to fight our fears
Brotha Rap is gone but he has left behind
A message that should wake up Wo-Hu-Man kind

FRED HAMPTON

I would not concede Brotha, just from looking at you
That Hanrahan could believe you were a threat to the Red
 White and Blue
And that punk William O'Neal, what kind of Brotha was he
Gave 'em the diagram, timeline, and put drugs in your herbal
 tea
The FBI, CIA, and Chicago PD
They had to sneak up on you, shoot you in your bed, in their
 line of du ty
Get up Fred Hampton and bust that MF in his face
Back him up against the wall, spray him with his partner's
 mace
Tell him your name, your stance, your rights as a hu man
Make him write it down so that his children understand
Back him out your door and make him come in right
Between 8am and 5pm in the daylight not 4hrs after
 midnight
Wake up Fred Hampton, lying on that mattress, bullet holes
 in your head
Wouldn't think to look at you that you were a threat like they
 said
They had to sneak up on you to shoot you and in your face
I cannot believe my Brotha, the things they did under their
 God's grace
Hanrahan made you a threat to the Red White and Blue
Exploited his position just to get rid of you

And that punk William O'Neal, what kind of Brotha was he
Gave 'em the diagram, timeline and put drugs in your herbal tea
Wake up Fred Hampton, wake up.

RODNEY KING

Rodney King got attacked by LA's Red White and Blue gang
They put their foot up his ass and kicked out his brain
As he lay there bleeding, he was heard to mumble in quiet refrain
Stammering, halting, insane gone, *can't we just all get along?*

NO!, Rodney King we cannot all get along!

HUEY P.

Now Huey P. didn't start out as a natural man
In the beginning he was a whisper, a will to hope, a wish to
 find
something worth living for
Then, the whisper put on flesh
His footsteps sounded across the world in a low cadence
like rhythm
African folks had an irresistible impulse to smile
Huey P. was everywhere, in full ebony armor
He lived and worked on the streets of Oakland and all the
African folks knew him in the flesh
You could recognize him by the stance he took and he
 delivered his message on the
rise of the times
He didn't call to the feet of those who were fixed against
 hearing him
No, Huey P. was an inside thing, a thing to live by
He was sure to be heard where the people were the poorest,
 where the police were the meanest, where racism cut
 the deepest
Sometimes he would be on the Westside when the lash of
 oppression fell on the Eastside,
but before the blood was dry on that African person's back
 he was there, coming nearer, then closer
The people knew something better was coming.
The establishment couldn't get the best of Huey P., he was
 unbeatable

He could beat them all, and what made it so slick he would finish it off with a laugh

Now, I hope you're not one of those "far removed" type folk, the kind that don't believe anything somebody tells them, the kind that done got ashamed of the things that brought us through.

That's why distance and the impossible had no power over Huey P. He had come from the streets of Oakland. He had come walking on the waves of revolution.

Wait now, it was no accident that Huey P. got by the eyes and ears of the enemy Folks.

Even them Folks that thought they understood, didn't understand.

That's because they were no longer looking for hope and it was not much of a strain for them to

find something to laugh about.

Huey P. was out of place for them.

But the truth of the matter is that the establishment

did understand him once or twice. They understood him making a way out of no way, hitting a straight lick with a crooked stick!

Man, Huey was deep! He had the wisdom tooth of the East in his head. Yeah, when troubles seemed too hard to bear, and the people didn't have a moment to spare, he would come around and say, *Hey now! Listen!*

He who wins from within is in the 'BE' class! You be here when the time comes, and your time will be here when you're gone!

GOD BLESSED AMERICA

God Blessed America, soil of enslaved, oppressed, unfree
Land of the melted pot, yo ho can you see
They say you must look like we, talk like she, walk like he
Think like   I should think not
My country 'tis of love it or leave
our children are dying and mothers grieve

Playas in wash and wear drip dry do it yourself coveralls
turn left, turn right 'cause you're wrong if you turn at all
Oh beautiful but spacious skies, filled with pollution
Enough to make you cry
There's the L A smog, the police and the dog
and where will we bury the trash
And there are people in our government who have a stick up
    their ass

America, America, God shed its grace on thee
While others shed tears, live in constant fears, scream and
    no one hears
And time is running out, oh beautiful purple mountain clout
Soaps are phosphate free from the last living Redwood tree
    and no more DDT
People, what a travesty!

Oh say can you see, past the pages of FOX, CNN, and NBC
Over the stacks of War Dead, under the blockade of bigotry

through all the mechanisms that distort us, into the lives of
	everyday people?
And if you do see, why in the fuck are you just sitting there

Nuts 'n Sand

I ain't one to talk. So you ain't heard this from me.
But this is the word as it was incurred, live at five USATV

Thousands of miles away on Saudi Arabia's row
Gotdam Whosaidso stepped on Isray Lee's big toe
After Endrun Chainme had told him no
Isray Lee looked up with tears in his eyes
Said *I'd fight you Gotdam but I've got an even bigger
	surprise.*
Lee chartered a boat, sailed across the ocean wide
His ship of State landed on the other side
Waded in sleet, skated through snow, washed up with the
	rain
On the Potomac's South Pacific sho

Told Iambush Baby in his own little faithful way
About Gotdam Whosaidso and what had happened before
	the passing of the day
He said, "Deep down in the desert where the tall oil rigs
	grow
A box-back, two-faced, wig wearing sucker was in the
	downtown square, putting on a show
Saying terrible things about your family, things I don't think
	you truly want to know

'Cause if he had said anything like that to me, you'd hear 'bout it, blow after blow
Yeah, he talked about your Country, Congress, and the House of Representatives too
In fact Bushbaby, he didn't show too much respect for you
Now, On your mama he went easy, concerning your grandma it was really bad,
But when he started talking about your daddy, that's when I really got mad!"

Iambush said, *What! This Gotdam Whosaidso sounds awful evil and mean*
I think I'm going to have to put together my daddy's war machine
He called for Condolease Foraprice, told her to summon the Army, Air Force, 8 Navy Seals, and a good Marine
Wake up Colon Pow Well, the Congress, the House of Representatives and Senate too. He had to have a talk about this unscrupulous couth.

They found Whosaidso sitting on an economic reef
Iambush Baby started yelling, *I'm the commander here, chief!*
See In and In continued to ask, *What's the beef?*
Congress stood under the spotlight shaking like a leaf.
Bushbaby told Gotdam *Ain't but two things standing between you and me.*
One is this desert sand, the other is that vast sea
I'll put my foot in your chest, slap you up side your balding head

Pull all the nails out of your fingers and tell your nasty greasy looking Mama, everything I said.

Gotdam looked down, tilted his head to the left side, caught a glimpse of Iambush out of his corner right eye
He said *all right now Bushbaby, I ain't gon tell you no lie*
Your brother is a beer guzzler and your daughters ain't no mom and apple pie...
Iam didn't listen, he wound up and swung from the ground
Had no doubts in his mind Whosaidso, Gotdam was sure to go down
Gotdam stepped back, spun around, and ducked to the right
Kicked Iam with a left foot and that's what really started the fight!
They fought up in the mountains, they fought in the valley low
The media in them Baghdad hotels were calling it blow for blow.
They fought during the day. They fought during the night
I still don't see how Iam got out of that fight
But he dragged on off to U inn's third round bell
Said something, mumbled something about not feeling real well

He was sitting in his corner looking more dead than alive when Isray Lee leaned over him, it was obvious, he was about to backslide
Lee looked down, and with a sigh of anguish and grief
Said, my Lord, my Lord what is this beat-up mess I see?
Is that you, Bushbaby? Jesus Christ do tell! Your nose is flat

and your eye is about to swell?
And he's still over there talking about all his vast oil wells!
You're getting beat up man. I mean he's done jumped all in your stuff!
You're supposed to be the world police. Is all that talk just a bluff?
Now the last thing I heard, Whosaidso was talking about your other niece
Something about her and that pipe, unrelated to Indians and peace."
Now wait a minute you big overgrown bureaucrat don't you glare!
I'll slap you in your face and pull out the rest of your hair!

Lee started laughing, moonwalking, and spinning all around
Feet got tangled up; he tripped and fell to the ground
Baby was on him along with the whole Navy's Sixth Fleet
Told Lee, *I'm gonna whup you mutha dusta from your head to the bottom of your tiny little feet.*
Isray Lee looked up, you could see the fear in the whites of his eyes
He started begging Bushbaby to allow him to apologize
Said, *Get your foot off my neck brotha, let me get my nuts out of this sand!*
I'll step up in this ring and fight you like a natural Afghan!
Iam called off the Army, Air force, 8 Navy Seals, told his good Marine to "stand down!"
'Cause this was the last time Lee was going to make him look like Homey da Clown
Iam stepped back to let Lee make his play, Bush intended to

whup somebody's ass that day.
Isray jumped up made a mad dash for the U inn's door
He was heard to shout loudly, long before either foot touched the floor
Your grandfather was a punk, your wife a sophisticated bore, and if you mess with me again, I'll have Gotdam whip your ass some more!!!
Well they tell me it was sight for sore eyes and blind people to come and see
But you know, I ain't one to talk! So you ain't heard this from me!

JIM CROW

Jim Crow on the edge of repeat
The Elite on the rise
I can only surmise
You can all see what lies
Under the political disguise
Or are you part of this demise

BACK PORCH

If you can't run with the Big Dogs
You had better stay on the back porch

ROUND MIDNIGHT

Round one: having lots of fun, ought to go home 'fo the morning come
Round two: feeling brand new, party don't start 'til they get past you
Round three: morning in the wee, don't leave now all we drinking is tea
Round four: a body at the door, music too loud, neighbors in an uproar
Round five: trying to keep it live, everybody fading, party in a nosedive
Round six: I need me a fix. You say all you got is that head nod shit
Round seven: I know that ain't the Reverend. Collar turned around, getting seven come eleven
Round eight: Came to work late. Boss in the doorway looking real straight
Round nine: I'm not feeling fine. Staying out late must be outta my mind
Round ten: Got a call from a friend, talking loud 'bout doing it all over again
Round eleven: I put it to you brethren, keep this up, you'll never get to heaven
Round twelve: Seeing green elves, head keeps ringing "round midnight, hell!"

JAZZ IS

Jazz is something I ought to know
Jazz is the first time I heard Betty Carter, and didn't dig her
All that, bee bop beeee bo bo ba bop
And so loud
I had to almost shout when I ordered my drink
You know, it was that kind of place
When the set ended, I was somewhat puzzled
"What it is?" I said to the Cat next to me
Maybe I ought to split
And he said, "Sit!" Jazz is something you ought to know
Anyway, she got back too soon and started scatting again
Man! I paid extra just to get a good table right down front
Where I could be seen
"Hey my man," I said, "don't this sound strange to you?"
Geez, now she had him bee bop beeee booing too.
Maybe jazz is something I ought to know, I said
She was making that same sound when I first came in
He said, "for MILES she blows, so COLTRANE will know,
Its DIZZY'S CHARLIE PARKER show."
And I kept wondering,
There must be something, jazz is, that I don't know
This time she started that be bopping in my direction
Really grabbed my attention
And there I sat
Waiting, watching, wanting to understand what jazz is
Damn, I almost heard something that time

TAMARA & JAY'S NEW ADDITION

Where'd y'all git dat baby from?
Don't try n' tell me she came out through that gaping door
Ain't nobody come through all that drama and trauma
    looking that good
dat I seen before

So where'd ju git dat baby from?
Don't lie now, I'm a wise old man.
Yesterday I was over at the Milpitas' dollar store
Was that her hidden behind door number four?

Where y'all be shopping, Wal-Mart?
I know they had a sale on the other day.
But dat stuff they be pushing,
I wouldn't buy even if it was me they'd pay.

Where'd jugo? Was it Macy's?
You know they tried to go bankrupt awhile back there.
They may not be around when you try and return her
'Cause she done lost all her hair.

And that pink hat, I saw it over at the Great Mall
In Burlington coat factory store.
I tried to git one myself
But the police stopped me at the door.

Where you git that baby from?
That's right, I know
And the Stork told me
She ain't delivered nothing to yo' front door.

Don't lie to me,
'cause Barbie don't make dem dolls look like that.
You done stole somebody's child.
You better give it back.
You bought it at Niemen Marcus?
OK, San Francisco Bloomingdales fifth floor?
Couldn't have been Eastridge
'Cause you don't shop over there no more

Come on now
Where'd y'all git that baby from?
Don't try to fool an old man like me
I was in and around before either of you turned three

She's too pretty
So I'm gon investigate this case myself
And when I find out where you got her
I'm gon arrest you for Grand Larceny and Theft

So you'd better tell me
Tell me quick
'cause neither one of you
Is that smooth and slick

Where'd ju git that baby from!?

DAVID PIPER

I WENT TO COLLEGE

College ain't so much where you been as to how you talk
    when you get back
Anybody can do it, look at me

There is a whole lotta things about this human question we
    ain't never thought of
Cultures are split like a fat man's underwear and somebody
    besides the supreme court has got to make a stand for
    the everlasting glory of people

Snatch humanity from the jaws of discourse and filibuster
Put thunder back in the schools and curriculum and
    righteous indignation back in the halls of Science

Make educational rights from educational wrongs and bring
    that whole baggage of canon fodderism to a fair and
    just conclusion

We must remind this elite and dominant structure that
    there ain't never been more than a fine line difference
    between one person and the other albeit race, gender,
    creed, or color, since
Aunt Ethel set the first batch out to dry

EASTERN SUN

Eastern Sun raise your prism
Shine it on these youth of today
Our daughters, sons, mothers, fathers
Deep within our hearts do stay.

Eastern Sun tell your story
gather all the young to hear
African proud crossing over
armed with knowledge have no fear

Got each gallant warrior's name
We are the soil from whence they came

So Eastern Sun in your splendor,
Take these children by their hand
Spread your glory, sunshine
Protect them from these harmful hands

                                    Unify us! Don't deny us!

   (Repetitious)

FOUR WOMEN

Machiko Kyoya

When you wake up this morning
Take a look at what I wrote
Just you, just me, always together
I made up my mind some 30 years ago
When I first saw you, I wanted to be in your flow
And it's amazing homegirl
How we have made this work
No matter what the challenge
We have faced them with pride
Our bond is our protection
And we don't have to hide
A thousand nights will past through our days
And we'll always be always together
Just you, just me
The years have turned our hair silver and grey
And the days of our youth are far far away
Golden, golden memories we will keep in our minds
The universe to us has been very kind
No matter what the challenges
We have faced them with pride
Our bond is our protection
And we don't have to hide

Requiem for a heavyweight Ayo (Thuy)

Ayo climbing ladders, I say hey, "What's the matter?"
    She say, "A train just ran over me."
    I say, "How often does that happen?"
She say, "Everyday I'm caught napping"

I say, "Well, hey you better come down from that step ladder."
    She say, "I cannot believe that's your chatter."
I say, "Your mind can achieve it, reach out and take my hand."
She say, "I don't know 'bout you brotha
You being somewhat the other, You just might not really understand."

I say, "Everybody climbs ladders
I can tell you what's the matter
There's an elephant in the room uprooting your tree."
She say, "How often does that happen?"
I say, "When the train is clippty clapping."
She say, "See, you don't know nothing 'bout me."

I say, "Well tell me Ayo
What's the name of your game?
Why is it a letter to the T?"
She say, "You freak, of what trains and elephants do you speak?"

I say, "The ones that ran over you and uprooted your tree"

She say, "Far into the matter, I've got to climb this ladder
 and height doesn't frighten me.

When twitter becomes twatter, when splitter becomes
 splatter, and I have achieved the tenth ring on the
 ladder
You can reach out and take my hand then you'll understand
 ... Everything is alright with me, after me.

Shuri (Rebecca)

Do what you want to do
So much enlight for you that's new
Free what you see you want to be
Be strong and dwell through harmony
So many ways for you to choose
Some of them to win and
So many others to lose
People come and people go
The game we play is "I didn't know"
I see you looking for the translation of these words
A lexicographical bible that tells you what you just heard
Don't close your mind to what you can see
Can it be sung in G flat key?
Is it the truth that's really there?
Is it the game we make up that we call fair?
Somehow, we all must walk our own path

Yokoye (Yolanda)

Take some time
    But there is still a limit
When life shows up, you've got to be in it

A child in core seeking detachment from hibernation
    A release of consternation the woes of education
Even when they tell you It's sophistication.
Just like any ol' playa all you need is good observation

Time needs to be a little longer
    The greetings need to be a little stronger
They tell me the answer is take your time
    I say phone calls used to be a dime

I GOT JOKES

Peter Peter was a punk ass cheater
    had a lovely wife, but he always beat her
    smacked her twice upside her head
    she fucked him up after they went to bed

My Uncle Sam got himself in a jam with the F.R.B. I-O
Went to the Well, the Fargo sale, bought himself a dope boat
Put some dope over here some dope over there
Here dope, there more dope, everywhere rope-ona-dope
My Uncle Sam is now on the lam from the BCC you know

Little Miss Misfit
Wants to hang wid the big chicks
Mad 'cause she can't go out today
Along came Granmah Ida
Sit on the bed beside her
Said, "girl don't make me go git that switch"

Humpty Dumpty climbing Great Mall's walls
Impudence, insolence of all the gall
His foot missed a step it was a terrible sprawl
All of his relatives and some of his best friends
Said I bet chu he won't be doing that shit again

SONG ON

JALIYA! Guardian of the Word!
Sing us your song 'O Halekulani with Al Kebulan of the past.
With your voice we echo the first, with memories of the last
I am Jaliya's, guardian of the word.
When it comes to the listener, I am the first one heard.
The Jembe (Jim bay), Gankogui (gang koh goo ee), Axatse
   (ah hah cheh) sing my song
Relax, sit back, this won't take long.
Listen, and you will hear many things of yesterday.
By this time tomorrow I will be far, far away.
I am Jaliya's guardian of memory and history.
Keeper of the word that unfolds the mystery.
Many a generation have come and gone
Many a generation have heard my song.
As I will speak of all things that came to be.
You will listen and see even more clearly.

DRUMMER'S SON

On the corner of Fulton and Masonic
All dressed in black, down to his patent leather pointed toed
 shoes.
Leaning up against the School of Education Building at the
 University
Feet planted, jembe resting on his left-hand side.
This steadfast, blunted head, confident man of these times
Hears the voices of all African Americans call out
We all supposed to be dead, but we ain't
He picks up his drum and moves on

TRIBUTE

I have been fortunate to have two of my all-time favorite persons in my life, Dr. Anita P. DeFrantz and Dr. Emile Wilson, Faculty at University of San Francisco. I want to thank Dr. Wilson for pulling me out of that elevator on that most critical day that I let fear override my good judgement. I boldly applied for the Doctorate program at USF and was accepted. When the moment arrived and the first day of class was upon me, I panicked and decided not to step off the elevator. Dr. Wilson was on that elevator and gently nudged me forward while dispelling my fears by saying, "...you belong here, just keep walking."

I want to thank Dr. DeFrantz for supporting me in so many ways and for cultivating a "never say die" spirit that brought me this far. I will never forget the helpful guidance, assistance, understanding and friendship that has been given me. Starting with the very first courses of instruction given by each, I have been challenged both intellectually and academically. For as my Great Great Grandmother would have said from the translucent four cornered walls of her room, "all things are possible, nothing is absolute, and everything happens in time, 'cause ain't no Great Great Grandmother in this world gon leave their Great Great Grandchild here ignorant!"

I will forever be indebted to my wife for her strength, understanding and willingness to face this challenge with me.

ABOUT THE AUTHOR

David Piper, Ed.D. has had years of experience as a Community Theater Director/Performer, curriculum developer, project/program manager and college instructor with an analytical, intuitive, expressive instructional style. He is an active participant in Multicultural Arts Leadership Initiative (MALI), a program designed to develop and deliver emerging multicultural art leaders. He has a Doctorate in International Multicultural Education, and Masters in Counseling Education. He has studied with Dr. Willie Williams in African American Theater at San Jose State University, Dr. Hal Todd in American Theater at San Jose State University, Master drummers Babatunde Olatunji - Eslen Institute; Molunga Casquelourd - Fua Dia Congo; Dr. CK Ladzepo, Ethnomusicologist - University of California, Berkeley, California; Dr. Zak Douf - Molunga Casquelourd Art Center, Oakland California; Royal Hartigan, San Jose State University; all of which have contributed highly to his management, presentational versatility and performance style.

www.ingramcontent.com/pod-product-compliance
Lightning Source LLC
Chambersburg PA
CBHW072020290426
44109CB00018B/2298